THINK LIKE
SHERLOCK HOLMES

How To Improve Observation & Deduction,
Solve Problems, Make Smarter Decisions, &
Become A Genius In Any Skill

(MASTER YOUR MIND)

Table of Contents

Introduction

Introduction

The methods explained in the following pages have worked for countless people and if followed properly will drastically increase your intelligence.

I have laid out the techniques in simple, layman's terms. You do not need to be a genius to follow this program or even have any sort of background.

You should read the chapters as they are provided to you, one after the other. The first chapters gives you vital information about intelligence and the human brain, it is important that you go trough this information before starting any of the actual techniques.

Read on and start improving your quality of life today. My personal advice would be to read through all the content before starting the program as you might find something you like a bit more later on. Also, when you understand every element of the program, you can utilize it more fully. Always keep the bigger picture in mind and try to visualize everything before you get to it.

The Brain

Chapter 1

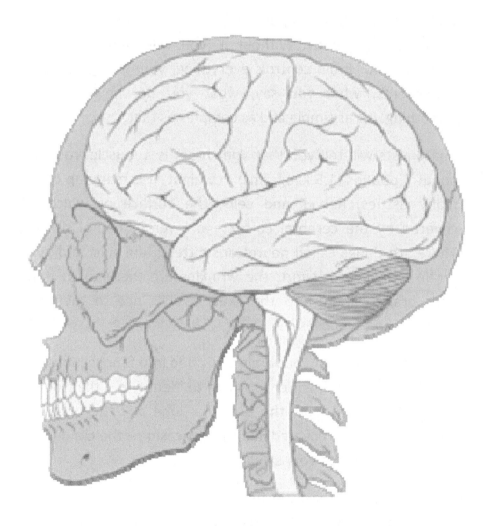

The Brain

So what is a brain? What is it made of, and why is it such an important organ?

Well, first of all, it's important because it is in essence the engine of your body. Without it, you will simply cease to function. Your brain controls everything, your thoughts, your movements, what you say, what you do, how you do something. It's as simple and as complex as that.

Anatomists will tell you that your brain is a muscle, roughly about 3 pounds (1.5 kilograms) in weight. It is made up of so many tissues, nerves and cells, the surface of which is covered by the cerebral cortex – a layer of neural tissue. There are things called neurotransmitters; and sulci and gyri (brain wrinkles for short; the wrinkles are there to so that your brain will fit into the skull easily); not to mention neurons, and synapses.

You will find out that your brain is divided into four sections by scientists to make it easier for them to identify it – the frontal lobe, the parietal lobe, the temporal lobe and the occipital lobe; and that it is covered in a thick encasing – the cranium – otherwise known as your skull.

You will also find that your brain is very fragile, in spite of the guards set up around it to prevent it from being harmed.

You will find out that shaking a person's head violently can lead to severe damage as the brain is shaken inside the skull.

(Interestingly enough, it should also be noted that the "grey matter" that you might have heard about, is really a pink-beige color.)

All that said, it is most interesting to know that your brain, this fragile, 3 pound organ, is the one thing that is running the show. Without, we would simply cease to exist.

Interestingly, many of us don't consciously tap into the full potential of our brain. Science has yet to discover all the wonders of the brain. But if you are willing, you will find that you can tap into the vast power that your brain has, and come out the winner.

Brain Potential

Chapter 2

Brain's Potential

Have you ever lost your glasses and been unable to find them?

Have you ever been caught out at a shop because you weren't quite quick enough to calculate the total?

Have you ever wished that you could work the crossword puzzle or Sudoku faster?

Well, by training your brain to harness its full potential (or at least, more then you are currently harnessing from your brain), you will find that it becomes easier to overcome hurdles such as these, so read on and find out ways of using your brain to its fullest potential possible.

Harness your brain's potential

Your brain is a unique organ. It can do many wondrous things that you can only dream about, but the truth of the matter is that the brain is capable of doing virtually everything. You only need to learn to harness more of the potential of your brain to do this. Now, although this might sound simple, it's not really all that simple. You will have to spend at least a couple of months unlearning all those unfortunate mind-numbing things we have learnt over the course of our lives (such as sitting for hours on end watching TV).

In order for us to harness the power of the brain, we need to make it work. And in order to make it work, we need to give it challenges. It needs to be exercised. And yes, you also need to give your brain time to rest and rejuvenate. All of these things are necessary if you want to harness more from your brain.

By following this program, you will benefit from enhanced brain capability – you will learn how to focus your mind, to use your deductive reasoning, to figure things out from only a handful of clues. Your memory will improve, and you will find that the world in general is an easier place to handle with a better functioning brain to solve the problems or tasks that we face on a daily basis.

In essence, what you get from this program is a shot at training your brain the right way; the way in which we were never taught while we were growing up.

You don't need to pop a magical pill or go to any extreme lengths in order to get your brain under your control and working in tip-top condition. All you need to do is to discipline your brain to work the way you want it to.

Testing Your Intelligence

Chapter 3

Testing Your Intelligent

There are many, many ways and means of testing ourselves, whether it is through exams such as we used to do when we were still of school going age, or whether it is through sporting events. We pit ourselves against other people and strive to not only come out on top but also to test our level of intelligence, our level of ability to do something or perform some feat.

It is a well known fact that the current educational system (School, College, and University) is more based on memory, instead of actual intelligence. By this it is mean that if a student has a somewhat good memory, he will do great in exams because he can simply memorize everything. However, when this same student faces common tasks that require "actual intelligence", he might not do as good because he never trained to use his intelligence, but simply memorized everything.

Obviously, the above does not apply to everyone. There are many students that boost a great memory as we as a great intelligence level, however, memory and intelligence are two different things and one can exists without the other.

Testing our intelligence is best done through properly formulated intelligence examinations instead of through examinations say on mathematics or literature, or something else along those lines. The reason for this lies in the fact that intelligence examinations have been formulated with the specific need of measuring the Intelligence Quotient of a person; hence the "IQ Test" that we are all familiar with.

So, how do you go about testing our IQ? Well, there are many methods of doing this, but one of the easiest ways is by going to this website and doing the IQ test found there:

What do you do after you take the IQ test? That's also quite simple. You take the IQ test then you come back here and keep reading the next chapters, to help you boost up your IQ. Remember, the brain is an ever-evolving organ – the more you use it, the better the results.

And one last thing before we leave you to get on to your IQ test: if you have kids, or are in the middle of doing something, such as a project or cooking up a masterpiece, then you will not want to get into the IQ test just yet. When you take your IQ test you will want to be in a calm environment where no outside influences can disturb your train of thought.

Moreover, you need to do the test at the appropriate time when your brain is most lucid. The first thing in the morning (Just waking up) or the last thing in the afternoon (Tired after a day at work) is not the best time to do such tests.

Considering the above, it is also important to note that IQ varies depending on your tiredness. If for example you are tired, you will not reason as much as if you were not, thus you would do badly in an IQ test in this state.

Brain Facts & Fiction

Chapter 4

Brain Facts & Fiction

So, now that you have finished your IQ test (or have planned some alone-time to get down to it later), let's find out some interesting facts about your brain.

- **Fact 1**: Your brain weighs in at (roughly) about 3 pounds (1.5 kilograms). This is an average figure and will change from person to person. For instance, did you know that Albert Einstein's brain weighed 15% more than the average person? So, depending on how frequently you exercise your brain muscle and give it stimulus, your brain can either grow, or like any other muscle, it can deteriorate without use.

- **Fact 2**: Your brain controls your entire central nervous system. This is what helps you to walk, talk, run about, do acrobatics, play chess, cards, and video games to name but a few things.

- **Fact 3**: A larger brain does not necessarily mean that you are smarter. It all depends on how you use your brain. For instance, Suzy has a lager brain but spends her days watching endless hours of TV she; Jane on the other hand, has a smaller brain than Suzy, but she spends her time reading, playing chess, doing sports etc.

Of the two of them, Jane with her smaller brain is going to be smarter simply because she is using her brain more and keeping it active. Suzy, although she has the lager sized brain, is putting her brain into neutral every time she sits down in front of the TV, which in turns prevents her brain from being utilized to its full potential.

So, although a larger brain can mean that you have an above average potential of intelligence, unless you frequently use your brain, it won't mean anything.

- **Fact 4**: Although scientists in general don't tend to agree on any one thing, it has been widely accepted that humans as a species are more intelligent than any other species. So, does this mean that are human have the biggest brains?

Well, if you look at it in size, then no, humans don't have the bigger brain. For instance, the brain of a sperm whale weighs in at a whopping 17 pounds (7.8 kilograms) while ours is only 3pounds (1.5 kilograms). However, that does not make the sperm whale smarter than a human. So how does that compute?

Well, the fact of the matter is (and you might have already guessed this) the size of the brain only matters when taken in conjunction with the size of the species. So for instance, in a human, the brain size to body weight ratio is what counts.

In humans the ratio is on an average 1:50. In other mammal species (such as the sperm whale) the brain to body weight ratio is much larger at an average of 1:180.

So you can see that while the brain of the sperm whale weighs in at 17 pounds, in conjunction with its body weight, the brain is indeed smaller than the average human brain.

- **Fact 5**: You may or may not have heard the theory that your brain gets new wrinkles every time you learn something. This is a flagrant myth. Your brain does not get a new wrinkle every time you learn something new. Our brain wrinkles stay more or less the same throughout our lifetimes (with a few variations depending on circumstances, illnesses etc).

- **Fact 6**: You use only 10% of your brain. This is contested by many scientists today who consider this to be a myth. You do not use only 10% of your brain. Whether you are sleeping, eating, running walking, or simply sitting around thinking about something, you are using 100% of your brain. The neurons, neurotransmitters etc, are working at all times. There is no one portion of your brain which is left unused.

However, and this is where it all comes together, the average person harnesses only a small percentage of their full brain potential. Or as psychologist William James said *"the average person rarely achieves but a small portion of his or her potential"*. And the only way to reach out and tap this source of power is by training your brain.

- **Fact 7**: Another interesting fact about your brain is that is said to consume about a quarter of your body's total metabolic energy. Think about it, one fourth of all your energy is consumed by your brain to help make your body run smoother among other things.

Things You
Need to Avoid

Chapter 5

Things You Need To Avoid

There are many, many ways in which you can tap into the potential of your brain, and we will talk these methods in the following chapters. This chapter however, is dedicated to steering you clear of those things that you shouldn't do if you want to harness your full brain power.

To give you a little taster of what we are talking about, we have given you a short list of the items we will be covering in this section.

So, what you *shouldn't* do – in a nutshell,

- **Being Stressed**

- **Lose Sleep – On a Regular Basis**

- **Watch TV for Hours No End**

- **Alcohol**

- **Smoking**

Being Stressed

Being stressed is one sure fire for you to confuse your brain's synapses into firing the wrong ideas at you...at the wrong time. Stress brings down all types of problems upon you.

The best thing that you can do is to try to get rid of your stress. This can be done in many different ways, the chief of which is trying to get you into a relaxed mental state.

So, if you live constantly with stress, try and follow these simple steps to get rid of it:

1. Take the time to step back and look at the things that are causing you stress. Is it something that is outside your control? Is it something that someone else is doing? Or maybe it's something that you yourself need to handle but just hasn't found the time to do so. Whatever the cause, the first step to dealing with it is to realize that it exists and what the reason for this stress really is.

2. When you have done this, you can then set about trying to hit on a method of either getting rid of the stress, or learning to integrate the cause into your life so that you don't stressed over it (for instance, if your sister is the cause of your stress, it would be pretty difficult to completely get rid of the cause, don't you think?)

3. The next thing that you need to do, is to try and focus on getting yourself relaxed. For instance, you should try and schedule a day (if you can manage it, or even a few hours is good), just for yourself. Do what you like best. Lie around in bed all day, watch reruns of bad TV programs eating cereal out of the box, go shopping, go to a spa, go nature hunting, indulge in photography. The point here is to help you relax and you need to find the best way for you to do that. This will be the first solid step in boosting your brain power.

And when you come back to your life from your little time out, what then? Well, the world will still be there, all the factors that went in to making you stressed, will more than likely still be there, and there will be more things just lurking around the corner waiting to stress you out more.

The trick is in learning to handle them. Deal with the ones that you can control and try very hard to make the ones that you can't control, slide alongside your life without impinging on it too much.

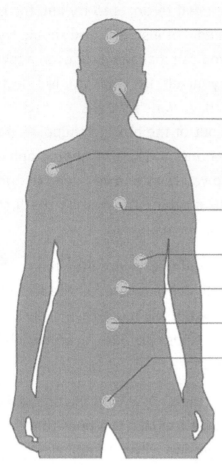

BRAIN AND NERVES
Headaches, feelings of despair, lack of energy, sadness, nervousness, anger, irritability, increased or decreased eating, trouble concentrating, memory problems, trouble sleeping, mental health problems (such as panic attacks, anxiety disorders and depression)

SKIN
Acne and other skin problems

MUSCLES AND JOINTS
Muscle aches and tension (especially in the neck, shoulders and back), increased risk of reduced bone density

HEART
Faster heartbeat, rise in blood pressure, increased risk of high cholesterol and heart attack

STOMACH
Nausea, stomach pain, heartburn, weight gain

PANCREAS
Increased risk of diabetes

INTESTINES
Diarrhea, constipation and other digestive problem

REPRODUCTIVE SYSTEM
For women-irregular or more painful periods, reduced sexual desire. For men-impotence, lower sperm production, reduced sexual desire

IMMUNE SYSTEM
Lowered ability to fight or recover from illness

Lose Sleep – On a Regular Basis

Insomnia, lack of sleep, sleep deprivation. Ultimately they all come down to the same thing: you are not getting the necessary hours of sleep for your brain to recharge.

Catnapping in the middle of the day does not count – although it does help for a quick recharge. If you want to look at it this way, it's a bit like charging in your phone for 5 minutes when the battery is almost dead. You'll get a quick boost that will last for a very short period of time before you find that you truly need to plug it in for a full recharge session.

So get the sleep, and remember to get the right amount of sleep. Although there is no doubt at all that you can survive on four hours of sleep, you want to do more than survive. You want to live, and you want your brain to be at its active best while you do so.

So if you suffer from insomnia – other than self induced down-at- the-pub-binges, all night book reading sessions, or marathon TV sessions – then you need to find out why.

Is it because your routine before you go to bed is disruptive? Do you have too much on your mind to fall into sleep? Or is it something to do with your heath?

Whatever the reason you need to find out. And the only reason you should be taking pills to help you deal with your sleeping problems is if it is doctor-recommended and has something to do with your health.

Barring that you will find that there are a number of things that you can do to help you get your sleeping pattern back to normal.

This includes, but is not limited to:

1. Putting on some tranquil, soothing, sleep inducing music as you get ready for sleep, and letting it run for some time.

2. Staying away from the TV for at least a half hour before you go to sleep. Actually, if you want to get picky about it, this includes the computer as well, and any other similarly brightly lit devices that will have you staring at it. The reason behind this is due to the bright light transmitting signals to your brain that it's not really dark outside and that it's not time for you to fall asleep yet.

3. Doing anything high paced, or well, active just before you get ready for bed. This is one sure fire way to wake up your mind.

4. . Eating a heavy meal just before going to sleep is also a great way for you to feel uncomfortable lying in bed. Eat your meals at least one to two hours in advance of your bed time. This will help everything to go down more smoothly.

5. Have you ever heard the phrase "Early to bed, early to rise, makes a man healthy, wealthy and wise"? Well, there was a reason this saying was popular, along with

the likes of "The early bird catches the worm". Not that you want to catch a worm, but you will find that earlier you can drag yourself off to bed – and make it a regular event, not just a once-a-week thing – the better you will feel. You will be more able to face the morning, and best of all your brain will be sharper and clearer.

6. And last but most definitely not least, you should really have a routine for going to sleep. That's right, a routine. Do the same things every night before going to bed. Over time, this will signal to your brain that it's time for you to hit the sack, and just like that, your brain will start shutting down for the night.

7. Another good panacea for insomnia, happens to be fresh air. Take a gentle walk – gentle, not strenuous – half an hour before going to sleep, or if you can handle it, you should try to keep the windows open, at least cracked open a little bit. This will circulate fresh air into your bedroom, and fresh air does wonders to make you feel better, more refreshed, even as you sleep.

Effects of
Sleep deprivation

- Irritability
- Cognitive impairment
- Memory lapses or loss
- Impaired moral
  judgement
- Severe yawning
- Hallucinations
- Symptoms similar
  to ADHD

- Impaired immune
  system

- Risk of diabetes
  Type 2

- Increased heart rate variability
- Risk of heart disease

- Decreased reaction
  time and accuracy
- Tremors
- Aches

Other:
- Growth suppression
- Risk of obesity
- Decreased
  temperature

Watch TV for Hours No End

In this TV run society that we live in, it is all too easy to forget that there is a world beyond that square box with the odd characters and odd sounds coming out of it.

It is also, all too easy to get sucked up into sitting in front of the TV for hour after endless hour watching one TV program after the other.

At some point you need to call a stop to watching TV, and maybe only watch it as a treat to yourself. Watch only the one or two shows that you *really* enjoy. Skip the ones that come before it, and after it if you only watch them because you are seated in front of the TV. You will be amazed at the amount of time this opens up for you.

Another good thing that you can do, is to eat your meals *away* from the TV. The temptation is all too irresistible to sit down and just catch a quick glimpse of this fascinating box full of such wonderful sights, sounds, and colors. Give your brain time to enjoy the fuel you are putting into your body.

Alcohol

Another big no-no in your efforts to boosting your brain power is alcohol. Alcohol once in a while, on social occasions is generally alright. After all, there are some occasions where you simply cannot avoid the obligatory drink. However, if you drink more than on social occasions, if you like to have a glass or two to unwind each day, then you might want to think twice about this habit.

You don't have to be an alcoholic for the effects of alcohol to dim your brain's functioning powers. Regular consumption of alcohol is simply bad for you. You lose all sense of inhibition, your sensory perception is shot to pieces, your speech will be affected, your reflexes will be a thing of the past, and more importantly, your brain will be unable to function properly until the alcohol has been washed out of your system.

Smoking

Smoking is bad for you, plain and simple. And you didn't need the surgeon general's warning on that pack of cigarettes to know it either. There are a myriad of things that are plain unhealthy with smoking, but first and foremost, is cancer (oral, laryngeal, and lung cancer).

And remember this, unlike alcohol, smoking also effects the people in or around your vicinity. Inhaling second hand smoke is almost as bad as smoking itself.

Although you might feel good, clear and focused after smoking, you can be assured that the effect will wear off. In fact, research has shown that after this initial effect has worn off, the longer term effect is that of a lowered intelligence level. And you really don't want that, do you?

One can find many quit smoking methods today, which are free and easy to follow; given that you really want to do it in the first place. **There's real no excuse in not to quit smoking.**

You can find lot of information on how to quit smoking online from the below page:

Increasing IQ

Chapter 6

Increasing IQ

Now, this chapter is the one you have been waiting for. It is the one with all the meaty bits, the one that will help you to boost your brain power.

That said, it should be noted that no matter how much you go through any of the things mentioned below, unless you remember to stop (or avoid) doing the things mentioned in the earlier chapter, the results will not be the same.

Also, it should be mentioned, that you will get far better results if you also learn to feed your brain the food it needs, as opposed to the foods your body has learned to appreciate over the years (i.e. junk food of all kinds, frozen foods, processed foods etc are a big no-no when you are looking to boost your brain power).

Below is a list of the most effective ways that you can do to boost your brain power. Start slowly with these easy to do yet very effective techniques, and you will find that as time goes by your brain power benefits from a great boost:

- **Brainwave Entrainment**
- **Palming**
- **Mind Games**
- **Exercising**
- **Meditation**
- **Other Techniques**

Brain Entrainment

Brainwave Entrainment, or "brainwave synchronization" is the practice of entraining one's brainwaves to a desired frequency (for example, to induce sleep), by means of a periodic stimulus with corresponding frequency. It depends upon a "frequency following" response, a naturally occurring phenomenon where the human brain has a tendency to change its dominant EEG frequency towards the frequency of a dominant external stimulus. Such a stimulus may be aural, as in the case of binaural beats, monaural beats, and isochronic tones, or else visual, as with a dream machine, a combination of the two with a mind machine, or even electromagnetic radiation.

But that all sounds like techno babble. Surely there's a simpler explanation?

Brainwave Entrainment for Dummies

Very simply, listening to a CD with the correct frequencies can transport you easily and quickly to a meditative state, which can help to achieve personal growth and improvement. If you like the idea of getting all the proven benefits of meditation, without the self discipline and work normally required, brainwave entrainment is the best option.

You've probably read how brain wave frequencies vary according to mental state. Daydreaming and light meditation take place in the "Alpha" range of frequencies, for example. So if you listen to music containing beats at a frequency of 10 Hz it will feel very relaxing, because your brain will begin to follow this frequency and reproduce the rhythm in the music. You will automatically generate more brain waves at a 10 Hz frequency and enter a relaxed Alpha mental state.

States of Consciousness

- Beta (14 - 30 hertz) - Dominant rhythm when awake, alert or anxious, with eyes open.

- Alpha (8 - 14 hertz) - Relaxed alertness; normally is induced by closing the eyes and relaxing.

- Theta (4 - 8 hertz) - Drowsiness, first stage of sleep; not common in awake adults, but common in daydreaming children.

- Delta (below 5 hertz) - Deep sleep.

Meditation can stimulate these states. Sounds can as well. Listening to specific sounds is the principle behind brainwave entrainment technologies.

Research has shown that this same state of "brain synchronization" is consistently found in the brainwave patterns of highly intelligent, creative, and successful individuals. This state of synchronization is the ultimate goal of many mediators since it allows one to tap into levels of mental performance not normally reached in everyday life.

To get started with this technique you need to download the brainwave mp3s included with this program and listen to them for about 15-20 minutes each session, for 4-5 times per week.

The Tracks are as following:

- *Deep Learning*

- *Q Booster*

- *High Focus*

Deep Learning - The first track is used to help you absorb information better and learn new things faster. – It's the ideal choice when you need to learn something new from a book for example and need an extra push.

IQ Booster - The second track improves your overall Brain Power by simply listening to it. – It's the ideal choice when you need to relax and can afford to do nothing but listening to it, to improve your general Brain Power.

High Focus - The third tracks helps your be in a state of Alertness – Whenever you need to get to a state of high alert, this is the right choice.

Additional Tracks can be bought from several third party providers online.

Palming

This technique can give you a quick boost in intelligence when completed as well as long term when followed on a daily basis. It helps people with visualization, improves your memory, concentration, numeracy and creativity. And remember, the more relaxed you are the better.

Step 1: Make sure that you are seated at a comfortable table and chair.

Step 2: Take a few deep calming breaths before you start.

Step 3: Lean forward on the desk or place your elbows comfortably on your knees in front of you.

Step 4: Rub your hands together until you can feel some warmth being generated. Close both of your eyes fully.

Step 5: Carefully without putting any weight or pressure onto your eyes place your two hands over your eyes. You should be able to blink freely and without feeling as if there is weight against your eyes. The palms should form a cup which covers the eyes. Your fingers should lie on your forehead and the heel of the hand will rest on your cheekbones.

Step 6: Tense the muscles in your entire body. Slowly relax these muscles and feel yourself relaxing. As you relax you should see a wall of black or darkness against the lids of your eyes. The darker the wall the better, this means that the amount of darkness you see is an indication of your state of relaxation. Follow this technique for about 15 minutes at least 1 time a day.

To get the full benefit of this exercise you will need to do the palming exercise as often as you can.

Palming

Mind Games

There's a lot to be said for playing games – if they are the right type of games. Games and puzzles are a gateway for you to get your brain to work on a daily basis. And the best part of it? They're also fun once you sink your teeth into them.

Some of the best types of games to get your brain juices flowing include,

- Crossword Puzzles

- Sudoku

- Scrabble

Other alternatives include playing bingo, bridge, and the penultimate, chess.

Below you can find a link to a list of games that you can play online for free:

Bingo

That's right – play bingo! There might be better things that you can do in your life, but you might find that an interesting night spent playing bingo is just the thing to wake up your brain.

Chess

Chess, there's nothing quite like it. It either drives you quietly insane, or you learn to enjoy it. If you can get past the stage where you are tempted to throw the chess board with all of its pieces into the dirt at your feet, then you might find that you have a good thing going.

The trick to learning chess is to not stress yourself out. Everyone loses the very first few hundred games or so (well, maybe except for those chess geniuses!). You will win maybe a very few in these beginning first rounds, but if you persevere you will find that eventually you are winning as many games as you are losing, which will pretty soon translate into winning more than you are losing.

We realize that playing a game is not all about the winning or the losing, but chess is such a disheartening and frighteningly brainy game, that losing consistently can be a bit a of a downer. This is why it is important to know that losing your first few games is a learning curve. Without losing, you would never know whether the move you made was a good one, or whether your opponent's attention was simply elsewhere at the time!

Chess, if you can bring yourself to learn it, is one of the best mentally stimulating games around. There is nothing to beat trying to outwit and outthink your opponent.

Exercises

So, alright, exercise is probably the last thing that you want to do in your free time, but the benefits of exercise cannot be denied. Even if you can't stomach the thought of getting in some exercise for your body, try and do it for your brain. It has been proven that regular exercise is good for your brain.

Besides clearing away the cobwebs, it also promotes better focus, and in some studies the subjects also showed a marked improvement in their memory functions.

Swimming

Swimming is a great way to ease into the field of exercising. You get to set the pace, and the best part of it is that your body is supported by the water. This means that you place almost no stress upon your joints.

Running

This is one exercise that you will want to ease into. For one thing, you will need to get yourself the proper type of shoes. This is necessary to help absorb the impact that running will put on your knees.

Running however has many great benefits attached to it, and if you are interested in starting it up, you will want to start slowly and build into it. Don't try to run the marathon the very first time you set out (although there's a very good chance that it will seem like you're running the marathon!).

Basic Schedule

Week	Workout 1	Workout 2	Workout 3
1	Brisk five-minute warmup walk. Then alternate 60 seconds of jogging and 90 seconds of walking for a total of 20 minutes.	Brisk five-minute warmup walk. Then alternate 60 seconds of jogging and 90 seconds of walking for a total of 20 minutes.	Brisk five-minute warmup walk. Then alternate 60 seconds of jogging and 90 seconds of walking for a total of 20 minutes.
2	Brisk five-minute warmup walk. Then alternate 90 seconds of jogging and two minutes of walking for a total of 20 minutes.	Brisk five-minute warmup walk. Then alternate 90 seconds of jogging and two minutes of walking for a total of 20	Brisk five-minute warmup walk. Then alternate 90 seconds of jogging and two minutes of walking for a total of 20 minutes.
3	Brisk five-minute warmup walk, then do two repetitions of the following: • Jog 200 yards (or 90 seconds) • Walk 200 yards (or 90 seconds) • Jog 400 yards (or 3 minutes) • Walk 400 yards (or three minutes)	Brisk five-minute warmup walk, then do two repetitions of the following: • Jog 200 yards (or 90 sec) • Walk 200 yards (or 90 sec) • Jog 400 yards (or 3 min) • Walk 400 yards	Brisk five-minute warmup walk, then do two repetitions of the following: • Jog 200 yards (or 90 sec) • Walk 200 yards (or 90 sec) • Jog 400 yards (or 3 min) • Walk 400 yards (or 3 min)

4	Brisk five-minute warmup walk, then:	Brisk five-minute warmup walk, then:	Brisk five-minute warmup walk, then:
	<ul><li>Jog 1/4 mile (or 3 minutes)</li><li>Walk 1/8 mile (or 90 seconds)</li><li>Jog 1/2 mile (or 5 minutes)</li><li>Walk 1/4 mile (or 2-1/2 minutes)</li><li>Jog 1/4 mile (or 3 minutes)</li><li>Walk 1/8 mile (or 90 seconds)</li><li>Jog 1/2 mile (or 5 minutes)</li></ul>	<ul><li>Jog 1/4 mile (or 3 minutes)</li><li>Walk 1/8 mile (or 90 seconds)</li><li>Jog 1/2 mile (or 5 minutes)</li><li>Walk 1/4 mile (or 2-1/2 minutes)</li><li>Jog 1/4 mile (or 3 minutes)</li><li>Walk 1/8 mile (or 90 seconds)</li><li>Jog 1/2 mile (or 5 minutes)</li></ul>	<ul><li>Jog 1/4 mile (or 3 minutes)</li><li>Walk 1/8 mile (or 90 seconds)</li><li>Jog 1/2 mile (or 5 minutes)</li><li>Walk 1/4 mile (or 2-1/2 minutes)</li><li>Jog 1/4 mile (or 3 minutes)</li><li>Walk 1/8 mile (or 90 seconds)</li><li>Jog 1/2 mile (or 5 minutes)</li></ul>
5	Brisk five-minute warmup walk, then: <ul><li>Jog 1/2 mile (or 5 minutes)</li><li>Walk 1/4 mile (or 3 minutes)</li><li>Brisk five-minute warmup walk, then:</li><li>Jog 3/4 mile (or 8 minutes)</li><li>Walk 1/2 mile (or 5 minutes)</li><li>Brisk five-minute warmup walk, then jog two miles (or 20 minutes) with no</li></ul>	Brisk five-minute warmup walk, then: <ul><li>Jog 3/4 mile (or 8 minutes)</li><li>Walk 1/2 mile (or 5 minutes)</li><li>Jog 1/2 mile (or 5 minutes)</li><li>Walk 1/4 mile (or 3 minutes)</li><li>Jog 1/2 mile (or 5 minutes)</li><li>Jog 3/4 mile (or 8 minutes)</li></ul>	Brisk five-minute warmup walk, then jog two miles (or 20 minutes) with no walking.

	walking. • Jog 1/2 mile (or 5 minutes) • Walk 1/4 mile (or 3 minutes) • Jog 1/2 mile (or 5 minutes)		
6	Brisk five-minute warmup walk, then: • Jog 1/2 mile (or 5 minutes) • Walk 1/4 mile (or 3 minutes) • Jog 3/4 mile (or 8 minutes) • Walk 1/4 mile (or 3 minutes) • Jog 1/2 mile (or 5 minutes)	Brisk five-minute warmup walk, then: • Jog 1 mile (or 10 minutes) • Walk 1/4 mile (or 3 minutes) • Jog 1 mile (or 10 minutes)	Brisk five-minute warmup walk, then jog 2-1/4 miles (or 25 minutes) with no walking.
7	7 Brisk five-minute warmup walk, then jog 2.5 miles (or 25 minutes).	Brisk five-minute warmup walk, then jog 2.5 miles (or 25 minutes).	Brisk five-minute warmup walk, then jog 2.5 miles (or 25 minutes).
8	Brisk five-minute warmup walk, then jog 2.75 miles (or 28 minutes).	Brisk five-minute warmup walk, then jog 2.75 miles (or 28 minutes).	Brisk five-minute warmup walk, then jog 2.75 miles (or 28 minutes).
9	Brisk five-minute warmup walk, then jog 3 miles (or 30 minutes).	Brisk five-minute warmup walk, then jog 3 miles (or 30 minutes).	The final workout! Congratulations! Brisk five-minute warmup walk, then jog 3 miles (or 30 minutes).

The above exercises are not only good for your intelligence but obviously for your physical performance as well.

Gentle Exercises

If you don't think you can stomach the idea of getting in some solid exercise, you might want to try your hand at something easier. The type of gentle exercise we recommend here is designed to bring all your energies into focus, and is very much a type of meditation.

The good things about these exercises are that you don't need to try and focus your mind solely on your mind. You focus on the flowing movements and through these you bring your mind into balance, while at the same reaping the benefits of getting some exercise as well.

You can try,

- Yoga

- Tai chi

- Pilates

Meditation

This is another good method of boosting your brain power. Unfortunately meditation does require some effort on your part to bring your brain into focus and requires you to exert discipline to stop your mind from wandering.

However, if you are interested in using meditation as a method of harnessing your brain power, then you will need to start slowly and build your mind up to gain the most benefits.

Don't go into this thinking that you can conquer the world of meditation in one or two sittings. It will take at least five or six sessions before you will be able to bring your brain under your control.

Once you have mastered this art however, you will find that it becomes easier as you progress to bring your mind into focus at any time you need to.

Other Techniques

Reading

While meditation is good to help bring your brain into focus, reading is good to help make it active and to make it think. Reading anything will put your brain into the position of having to work, and by doing that, you are making sure that your brain does not fall into the trap of being lethargic.

Read anything and everything that you can get your hands one. It doesn't matter whether it's a 10 page novella, or a trilogy sized volume. Take the time out to read, and you will be stimulating your brain to think in new and different ways.

A Good Breakfast

There's nothing quite like eating a good breakfast to start off your day. We realize that there is really not enough hours in the day for you to accomplish everything that you need to, and that getting up those precious few minutes earlier just to eat breakfast simply does not sit well with you. However, if you can make the effort, if you can get up in time to have a fairly good breakfast you will find that your brain functions much better.

Like any good machine, your brain needs fuel to function properly, and a good breakfast gives your brain the chance to jumpstart itself it in the morning.

There are a number of foods that you can tackle in the morning if you don't have the time to sit down to a full breakfast, including fruits, oatmeal, eggs, and coffee. Of course, you don't need to eat all of that! Even one or two things can help you on your way to a better day.

Challenge Yourself

One of the best methods of boosting your brain power is doing something simple, like challenging yourself. You are breaking out of the mold you have placed yourself in all these years, and trying to do things differently.

Switch your right hand tasks to your left hand

One good example is switching the tasks that you do with your right hand (if you are right handed), and doing it with your left hand instead.

For instance, think about right now. You are holding the mouse in your right hand and clicking happily away. Your brain has gotten so used to doing this that it comes automatically to you – just like breathing. You come to your computer, turn it on, and just like that without even thinking about it, your right hand settles comfortably over the mouse, and before you know it, you're clicking merrily away.

So why not try switching, right now. Move the mouse over to your less dominant hand (the left hand in most cases), and try clicking and moving the mouse. Not so easy is it? You have to think before you actually make a move, and wait...don't go there – that's the button that closes down this window!

That was close, but you can see what we're saying, right? Doing something in a different manner, even something as simple as using your mouse makes your brain to *think*. It has to come out of cruise control and take an active part in what you are doing.

Do Two Things At Once – and be aware that you are
So what else can you do to make life challenging without going too far out of your daily routine?

Well, you might want to try doing two or three things at once. Now, I know that many of us do this on a regular basis, we routinely talk and toss a salad together, we listen to music while working on something. And this is alright, but how about jazzing things up a bit and doing something a little more...well...*more.*

For instance, you could go for a walk (or run whichever one you're more comfortable with) and keep track of the number of dogs who cross your path; or maybe the number of red cars that go by. Trust us, this will not always be easy. There are so many things around to distract the mind and the eyes, that it can be somewhat difficult to remember the exact number you stopped at last!

The one thing that we would not recommend in any way or manner is splitting your concentration when you are dealing with sharp objects such as knives and scissors, or when operating heavy machinery, or for that matter, even when driving your car. (Although that last one is something that too many of tend to do when we're behind the wheel.)

Take a Class...learn something new

This could be one of the most fun and easy ways of exercising your brain. Learning something new is always fun and exciting...when you are not forced to do it (i.e. going to school).

Well, you're an adult now and can pick and choose exactly what it is you want to do. And the best thing about it is that there are plenty of classes and courses out there now that are geared towards adult learning. They don't have to take you down into a specific field; they don't even have to be beneficial to your work. They just have to be something that you will enjoy, and stick with through to the ending.

A good example of something that you could learn would be a new language, or maybe the art of painting (even if you don't believe you have the knack for it).

The main thing that you need to remember is that you are there to jump start your brain cells into realizing their full potential, and learning new things is one of the best and easiest ways to do so.

If all else fails, you will find that you are having to exert yourself by meeting new people and dealing with new situations. Another good reason why you should air out your brain by learning something new.

On the other hand, if you don't have the time or prefer to go it alone, you might find that starting an online course is all that you need to get yourself going.

48

Learning to play chess is a very good example of how you can learn something new on your own, without heading off to a class. Or maybe you would like to take your learning a step further and do a project, such as building a bird house or a bird feeder.

There are plenty of do-it-yourself kits available these days and you will find that these are also an enjoyable way of boosting your brain power.

The important thing is to learn the basics of something new (No need to master the new subject), and if you pick a new subject, its very difficult to fail; because you will learn something for sure.

Memorize things just for the fun of it

Now, this might sound a little bit insane to you, but if you can take to memorizing things around you, you will find that your mind retains things more easily, and that your brain's potential jumps up a notch or two.

You don't need to go in for anything fancy, anything you can get your hands on to memorize will do fine, as you can see from the list we have made below.

For instance, you can memorize,

- Your week's shopping list
- The multiplication table
- The last names of your coworkers
- The phone numbers in your phone book

The list of things that you can memorize is endless. If you don't want to memorize mundane things such as grocery lists and phone numbers, then you can try something more exotic, like the word 'No' in fifteen different languages...just for the fun of it: No, Nein, Nyet, Nahi

Travel the world – or just your little corner of it

So alright, this might not be possible for everyone to do, but the fact remains that if you can manage to get out and about, you are stimulating your brain.

Traveling doesn't necessarily mean that you need to travel to far flung and exotic places. It can be as far as down the road. The trick is to keep your eyes and ears open. Don't just step out of the house and go with blinkers on from point A to point B. Take the time to notice the world around you.

Stop and smell the roses, notice the fat bees tumbling around the flowers, listen to the far off whine of a lawn mower, hear kids arguing just a little bit down the street. Take in the sounds of the cars as they whiz by you, listen to the gossip going on all around you as neighbors come out to chat.

As long as you are aware of your environment, as long as you are challenging your brain to *work*, to see and hear everything that's going on around you, you will be pushing your brain's potential higher and higher.

And if you can manage to make it to another country, city, or even town, you will find that the benefits to be had are far greater. In a new environment you will be forced to pay attention to everything going on around you, and this is probably one of the best things that could happen to you.

Nutrition

Chapter 7

Nutrition

If you read the first chapters, then you might remember that we said that the brain consumes about a quarter of your metabolic energy. This means that your brain needs energy (and lot of it!), and for the right amount of energy to get to your brain, you need to feed yourself.

Think of your body like a car. If you put fuel into your car, it will function properly. It will respond to your actions and move forwards (drive), and move backwards (reverse). If you don't put any fuel into the tank however, your car will not move, no matter what you do. Oh sure, you can push it, but that's sort of along the same lines as being hooked up to a machine that does all your functions for you.

Your brain is just like your car then. Put fuel in the tank and it will move and do whatever you want it to. Forget to put fuel in it, or just as bad, put the wrong type of fuel in it, and your brain will become sluggish, and just like your car it will fail to respond to you.

Ultimately what this means is that along with the things you should do, and the things you shouldn't do, there are also foods that you should eat to help your brain function to its optimum. These are what we are going to talk about in the following sections.

So what are the best foods for the Brain?

Fruits:
- Blueberries
- Avocado
- Pomegranates

Carbs:
- Brown Rice
- Oatmeal
- Beans

Vegetables:
- Leafy vegetables
- Garlic
- Tomatoes
- Olive Oil

Fish, protein etc:
- Eggs
- Fish oils
- Tuna
- Wild Salmon
- Oysters

Miscellaneous:
- Seeds
- Nuts
- Chocolates

Drinks:
- Tea
- Coffee
- Fruit Juice (Freshly squeezed)

Going through this list you might notice a few things, such as the fact that sugar is not mentioned here – all sugar that you intake when you eat these foods are naturally occurring sugars. There is no mention of refined sugars in this list at all.

Which of course brings us to our next point. You will also have noticed that hamburgers, pizzas, frozen foods, and other such processed and fast foods have not been mentioned in this list. This is because, if you haven't already guessed it yet, these types of highly refined, nutrient deficient foods *are not* good foods to feed your brain or your body.

Once or twice a month is probably alright, but the minute you start putting these types of foods into your body, it is akin to topping up your car with vegetable oil instead of petrol. Before too long without your even noticing it, the 'bad' fuel will get into your system and your brain and your body will start slowing down.

Carbs (Carbohydrates)

Although many fat loss diets advise you to stay away from carbs, the truth of the matter is that carbs are necessary for your body to be healthy. **But it's important to eat the right carbs** – the ones that will keep you feeling full and satisfied until your next meal.

These are the ones that will slowly release the stored up energy of the carbs into your system so that it gets a steady supply of energy without your having to resort to a sugar rush.

Brown Rice

And brown rice is one of the best types of carbs that you can have. It is a complex carbohydrate which perfectly compliments your attempts to not only stay healthy, but also to harness the potential of your brain.

Oatmeal

So alright, not everyone likes oatmeal, but it cannot be denied that a good bowl of oatmeal not only warms your body, but is also full of natural goodness. It is high in fiber and will keep you going through the day.

Beans

This is one source of nutrition that many people tend to forget in their desire to eat healthy. However, beans are a versatile supply of energy and have many vitamins and minerals not to mention the fact that they are also full of fiber and protein.

Fruits

Fruits are a delight to the body. They contain sugars naturally. You have no need to enhance their flavor with additional sugar, and if you are lucky and can eat tree ripened fruits, then you get an additional dose of goodness as these fruits have had the time to absorb nutrients into their flesh over the proper period of time.

Blueberries

Although these scrumptious little berries have been around forever (remember mom's blueberry pancakes?) it has only been recently that researchers have found out just how good these berries are for us. In fact the research is such that blueberries, along with a handful of other foods such as garlic, have been labeled as 'superfoods'.

So what can blueberries do for you? Well, to begin with you should have blueberries in its fresh form where possible. Don't go in for the sweetened or dried varieties as the nutrition quotient in these is just not the same.

Interestingly, while blueberries are thought to be good overall for your body, it has been shown that Blueberries also reduce the risk of Alzheimer's. They are also safe for people who are diabetic, have a low GI (glycemic index), and are also high in fiber.

Pop a few blueberries in your mouth whenever you need a pick- me-up or a quick brain boost. The natural sugars will help to get your sluggish brain moving faster.

Avocado

Avocados on the other hand, help your body to better circulate your blood. What this means for your brain is that it gets the blood it needs, when it needs it.

Pomegranates

The food of the Gods, and some people believe, the apple that brought such problems for Adam and Eve. All that aside however you will find that a handful of pomegranates has about the same affect on your brain as blueberries. They are also full of antioxidants which most definitely help your brain to function better.

And although eating the fresh fruit is always better than having your dose of pomegranates juiced, get them in any way that you can. Just remember that you don't need to add extra sugar to this sweet fruit – whether it's fresh, or whether it's in juice form.

For a light salad to help you get through the day, try this:

Take a bowl and set it to the side. Wash and halve the pomegranate. Make sure that you do not get any juice on your clothes as it will stain.

Take a small spoon, or using your fingers, take out the red/pink seeds. This is the portion of the fruit you are going to eat. The outer shell is inedible.

Put the seeds into the bowl you set aside earlier and when you are done, sprinkle a little lemon juice over them. Next, take a small onion (the red ones taste better), and slice it very thinly. Add to the pomegranate seeds in the bowl, add a dash of pepper for taste, and mix well.

You can eat it straight away, or as we prefer, let it sit for a couple of hours so that the flavors all blend in together.

(Incidentally, this makes it the ideal salad to take along with you to the office. It's tasty, it offers you the boost you need, and it doesn't make you feel sluggish and weighed down as you would do with a heavier meal. Round it off with a nice tuna steak and a cup of coffee, and you will be good to go!)

Vegetables

Another problematic area when dealing with nutritious foods is vegetables. Most of us these days have grown up on fast foods and ones that are high in starch. We tend to favor our sweet tooth, and stay religiously away from anything that even remotely resembles a green vegetable. Unfortunately, eating vegetables in any form is not only good for you, it also helps your brain to sustain its energy throughout the day.

Leafy green vegetables

This is why you want to start with something simple such as leafy green vegetables. These vegetables are packed full of iron (among other things). And in case you were unaware of it, iron helps us to overcome a lot of things and helps the brain to function properly.

For instance, iron deficiency has been linked with such things as low moods, fatigue, cloudy thinking etc. So include a good dose of leafy green vegetables in your diet and you will see the difference almost immediately.

Iron rich vegetables include spinach, chard, arugala, and kale to name but a few.

Garlic

We realize that you are not vampiric in anyway so there is really no reason to stay away from the garlic. The pungent smell of this superfood is really quite heady when prepared in the correct manner...and of course when taken in small doses!

To get the best effects of garlic, you should always look to the fresh stuff to liven up your kitchen; anything else is simply a waste of space and adds no extra nutritional value to your diet.

Tomatoes

Tomatoes are also considered to be good brain food. They are high in lycopene when they are cooked, an antioxidant which has known properties to fight against dementia.

Stir up a fresh tomato based Bolognese for a truly memorable home cooked meal.

Olive Oil

So alright, Olive Oil is not part of the vegetables group, but the way I see it, if you're going to add Garlic and Tomatoes to this group, you might as well add Olive Oil and go in for a swinging Italian meal at the same time!

So why do we want to add oil to our list of good foods? Simply because no matter how hard you try to get away from it, your body needs fats, just like it needs carbs. It cannot sustain itself properly on a low fat diet. And just like eating carbs, you need to have the right fats for your body and your brain to be healthy.

This means that you should stay away from vegetable oils, corn oils etc. Oils such as olive oil and nut oils, flax seed oil, and even avocado oil, are far better for your health than any of the others.

Fish; Protein etc

Fish has to be one of the best know types of brain food there is, and yet in today's mainly meat-eating society, it is also one that is heavily overlooked.

Eggs

To get started however, we'll take a look at that staple breakfast food: eggs. Eggs are not only a good source of protein, but they also contain the proper fats that we spoke about it the Olive Oil section.

So even if you don't have time for a proper sit-down breakfast in the morning, you might want to try taking the time to gulp down a simple omelet before you head out for the day. This with a fruit, or even some fresh fruit juice and a cup of coffee will make a good start to your day.

Fish Oils

Many mothers have fed their children fish oils over the ages, thankfully for us, the method of ingesting is now better than it used to be. You can get your daily dose of fish oils in harmless capsules which allow you to take the fish oils without ever having to taste them!

Although fish oils are not a substitute for eating fish, they can help to augment your diet.

Tuna

Tuna between two slices of bread is one of the staples of mothers everywhere. It is tasty and versatile, and thankfully, many kids love the relatively mild taste of tuna.

But what good does it do for you? Well, besides being an obvious and naturally available source of fish oils, tuna also has an abundance of Vitamin B6. What this means to you and me, is that you will have better brain health over time.

Wild Salmon

Fats are important for our brain to function better, and this fish is full of the best kind of fats you can get – Omega 3 oils. And although it is entirely possible to get your dose of Omega 3 oils through the whole fish oil method we talked about earlier, it is also true that there is no better way for you to get your nutrients than through a fresh source.

Just a few things you might want to keep in mind however when looking to include Wild Salmon in your diet. One, being that you should avoid farmed salmon wherever possible as for some reason it just isn't the same. And Two, be careful when shelling out money for Wild Salmon as some unscrupulous people like to make a quick buck by fooling the consumer – that would be you and me – by coloring the normal farmed salmon so that it takes on the bright pink hue of the fresh wild salmon.

Oysters

If you are allergic to shellfish then you might want to be careful about having oysters, but if you aren't then you have just come across one of the best food sources that is high in protein, selenium, and magnesium among other things. In other words, it contains all those things which are most good for the continued well being of you and your brain.

Miscellaneous

This section we have to confess contains one of our all time favorite foods, and frankly we don't know how we got so lucky as to be able to include this in our brain foods section. What are we talking about? Chocolate of course!

Seeds

Before we go on to the good stuff however, let's take a look at some of the better stuff...like seeds. Yes, we said seeds. You will find that seeds of all sorts are truly good for you. They contain essential brain foods such as fat, protein, magnesium, and Vitamin E among other things.

They are also a good way for you to combat those mid-morning energy slumps, and they are easy to carry around with you so you will never be short of something to munch on.

There are a number of seed varieties out there that you can nibble on, including flax seeds, sesame seeds, sunflower seeds, and even pumpkin seeds.

If you are interested in finding more you might want to go on down to your local health store and browse around some to find a seed that tastes good to you.

Nuts

Ah, nuts. The staple of many a squirrel and not for the likes of us, right? Wrong. Nuts, just like seeds are packed full of nutritional goodness, and having a handful now and then can help to keep your brain in tip top condition. (Although you should be careful not to go overboard and overindulge in these delightful delicacies!)

Nuts are a combination of complex carbs, fats, protein, and Vitamin E. They are also high in fiber, all of which just goes to show you that you can't do any better than going nuts for a short break.

If you do care to indulge in these nutty delicacies, then remember to stay away from the ones which have been overly seasoned or sweetened. If you do want something other than plain nuts, remember that you want something that will boost your brain power, not inhibit it, so go for the ones that are only lightly seasoned or sweetened. Of course, it would be much better if you could go with the plain versions instead.

> If you really like to go nutty once in a while, then why not try out these nut varieties: Almonds, Macadamia nuts, Cashew nuts, Hazelnuts, and Walnuts, to name but a very few.

And no, Peanuts are just not the same. For one thing they aren't truly a nut variety and for another thing, the fats these little nuts carry, is not of the good type for your brain.

Chocolates

Now we get down to the nitty gritty...the moment we have all been waiting for – the chocolate moment. (And for those coffee lovers out there, we'll give you a coffee moment a well!)

So, how does chocolate come to be on this list? Well, to begin with it has been found that chocolate is good for many things besides enhancing your mood and mellowing out a troublesome day.

Chocolates are – if you will pardon the pun – choc-full of goodness. They are full of fiber – especially the darker varieties which are simply all about cacao.

Next up, you will find that chocolate is also said to be packed with antioxidants. And of course the necessary jolt of caffeine is also found in your all-time favorite food, in – surprisingly enough – the correct amounts. (Kind of like Goldilocks – not too much caffeine, not too little caffeine, but just the right amount.)

Your brain will function much better now that you know all of this, right! Go on, take your chocolate break now and enjoy a brain boosting moment.

Drinks

Next, we take you to the last of our brain food sections – drinks. No, we're not talking the alcoholic variety here, but the normal everyday, thirst quenching, pass-the-time-at-work variety.

So, first up you probably know that water is a very good way for you to quench your thirst. Unfortunately most of us just don't like the taste of water (having been reared on sodas and milkshakes in our formative years, then having switched to tea and coffee in an attempt to appear grownup). This being the case, we are as a society very much dependant on these beverages, and luckily for us, research has shown that indulging us – in normal quantities – is not only alright, it is also quite, quite good for our health, not to mention our mental health.

Tea

First up, let's take a look at tea, that wonderful beverage that brought on the likes of the Boston Tea Party. (One wonders if there were cucumber sandwiches along with this particular tea party? Would the fishes have appreciated such an offering?)

To get back to tea however, you should know that tea – in all it's Camellia Sinensis varieties (Black, White, Green, Oolong, and Pu- er) – is good for you. It contains a lovely number of antioxidants, and you can always be assured of getting a nice calming feeling when quenching your thirst with this beverage.

Just remember not to indulge in those ready-made varieties – when it comes to tea, fresh is always better.

Coffee

Ah, now we come to real deal. Coffee. Even the name conjures up early mornings at the beach watching the sun come up.

So, coffee. It makes you chipper, and it definitely makes you chirpier. It also contains fiber, which is the whole point of it being good for you.

If you can make your daily dose of coffee to be anything other than the instant variety of course that would be even better. That said, to get the most out of your coffee the very last thing that you want to do is to add loads of sugar to your coffee. This might be the only way that you can drink this bitter brew, but if you can get yourself to the point where you only take a minimum of the sweet stuff, you will find that the benefits of having coffee are greatly increased.

(For more coffee laden facts, head on over to the next Chapter)

Fruit Juice (Freshly squeezed)

And last, but most definitely not least, we take a look at that good old standby – fruit juice. And when we're talking fruit juice, we mean the freshly squeezed variety that contains no sugar at all.

Obviously the better way to get in your brain boosting amount of fruits would be fresh without juicing, but if you don't have the time to go with the fresh fruit, then by all means go for the juiced variety. Just make sure that you don't throw away all that fiber goodness along with the seeds, and you will be fine.

A glass of juice and a handful of nuts or seeds is a great pick-me-up at any time of day.

Caffeine And The Brain

Chapter 8

Caffeine And The Brain

So, alright, you never in the world would have thought that researchers in any denomination would have found a happy connection with caffeine and your brain. But the truth of the matter is that they have not only done it, they have also shown exactly how caffeine and your brain interact.

The short version of the caffeine-brain connection

In reality it would be really confusing if we were to explain all the details about the ins and outs of why caffeine is good for you. But don't worry, we're also not going to pat you on the head and tell you to take our word on the fact that caffeine is good for you – we will give you the ins and the outs of it...just not in technical jargon that is hard to follow and puts you to sleep before you can get through one sentence. And you can be assured that no amount of caffeine in the world is going to keep you awake long enough to get through all that technical jargon!

The first thing that you should know however, before you jump for joy that you can now indulge in your caffeine addiction is that anything that is good for you, is good for you in moderation. This applies equally across the board to everything in your life. If you indulge – or rather overindulge – in something, even if it is good for you, you can be assured that there will be repercussions for you to deal with over time, if not immediately. What this means for you, the avid caffeine fan, is that although you can indulge in something like 2-3 caffeine filled cups a day, anything more than that is really pushing the boundaries.

So, let's see what's up with the effects between caffeine and your brain. Well, the first thing is an effect that you yourself will have noticed over time. When you drink a cup of tea or (preferably) coffee, your senses become more heightened, your brain is sharper, you are feeling more wide awake, and your general outlook on life has improved.

This is the non-scientific version of the relationship between caffeine and your brain. Luckily for us, this effect has also now been scientifically explained away for us to be able to indulge in a caffeine laden cup of tea of coffee once in a while.

Caffeine is a stimulant which means it stimulates our mind and our bodies –

1. It stimulates blood circulation.

2. It stimulates your central nervous system.

3. It stimulates the heart.

4. It stimulates your respiratory system as well.

5. Dopamine levels to your brain are increased.

What all this really adds up to is that even though caffeine in any form is not a long term method of boosting your brain power, it can be used in short doses to help you boost your brain when you need it the most. It will keep you awake and alert and it help your mind focus.

However, just be sure to keep your caffeine intake to small doses, or you could find yourself craving caffeine in a way that is not good for you.

Caffeine Beverages

The first thing that we would like to say is that the caffeine found in sodas and the like are not the type of caffeine effects you are looking for.

The best quick pick-me-up caffeine drinks that you can go for include (but are not limited to):

- Tea

- Coffee

- Espresso (quite, quite different from normal coffee)

- Cappuccino

- Hot Chocolate

Power Nap

Chapter 9

Power Nap

This chapter is not about any techniques to improve your intelligence on a long term basis; however it's a special technique that can be very useful if you know about it.

How many times in your life did you felt tired during the day and wished that you could press a button and be refreshed and with a lucid mind – just as if you wake up in the morning? Well, a power nap is the nearest thing to this.

A power nap is a short period of sleep, usually in the day time. Such naps may be taken when one becomes drowsy during the day, otherwise wants to feel awake later in the day.

A power-nap usually terminates before the occurrence of deep sleep or slow-wave sleep (SWS), intended to quickly revitalize the person.

It is well known that power-nap duration of approximately 18 to 25 minutes is most effective. For any additional time, the mind enters into the deep sleep cycle. People who regularly take a power-nap may develop a good idea of what duration works best for them, as well as which tools, environment, position, and associated factors help induce the best results.

Try It!

If you feel tired at work and require a quick fix, take a power nap and you will wake up refreshed and with a clear mind. But pay attention, a power nap should be done properly and for no longer than 25 minutes – just enough time so that your brain gets some rest. If you power nap for longer, most likely you will wake up even more tired than before (Because your brain will enter in the deep sleep phase - you need to avoid this!). Use your alarm clock properly to wake you up in time.

Caffeine Nap

A caffeine nap is just like a power-nap but is preceded by the intake of caffeine. The main idea is that caffeine in coffee takes up to a half-hour to have an alerting effect; hence a short power-nap will not be compromised if it is taken immediately after the coffee.

Therefore, take a cup of coffee just before taking a power-nap, it will not compromised your sleep and when you wake up you will be both refreshed by the power-nap as well as alert by the caffeine.

Conclusion

Conclusion

What can we say now that it's time to part ways? Shall we tell you that it's been fun... because it undoubtedly has. We always enjoy spreading what we know with other people, and in essence, isn't learning new things part of boosting your brain power?

That being the case, it might be time to quit while we are ahead and allow you time to soak in everything that we have talked about.

Just remember, your brain is an ever evolving complex organ. You need to feed it the proper foods, you need to give it time to rest, and you need to stay away from those things which are most bad for you...and your brain.

And along with that you also need to exercise your brain. Use it regularly and don't let it go to waste. Give it things to do, make your life more interesting, and overall, just allow it to grow and flourish.

Appreciate what you have, take the time to stop and smell the roses, take in a game of chess, eat with your left hand if you're right handed, and remember to challenge your brain every single day. Your life will be fuller if you do.

Remember that it's never too late to teach old dog new tricks... and your brain is one old dog that will never stop learning.

-------------------------End-------------------------

Made in the USA
Middletown, DE
04 November 2019